Welcome to Leadership
Practical Elements and
Requirements of Leadership

Other Titles from Karl Bimshas

"An Unusual Year"
"Give a Damn"
"Leaders Don't Shrug"
"Go Get It!"
"How to Stay When You Want to Quit"
"Pushing Back the Ocean"
"How to Fix Your Whine at Work"
"Quick Ways to Be a Good Leader"
"Don't Be the A-Hole on The Team"
"So, I've Been Thinking"
"So, I've Been Thinking Some More"
"Think Again"

Welcome to Leadership
Practical Elements and Requirements of Leadership

Karl Bimshas

BimMedia

San Diego, California

Copyright © 2021 Karl Bimshas

All rights reserved. This publication or any portion thereof may not be reproduced or used in any manner whatsoever without the express written permission of the publisher except for the use of brief quotations in a book review or scholarly journal.

First Printing 2021

www.KarlBimshasConsulting.com

ISBN 979-8-496-18644-5

Dedication

For aspiring and new leaders. Remember, it is not the body's size, age, color, or gender, but what emanates from the soul that makes the leader.

Table of Contents

Introduction	9
Leadership Principles	13
Popularity, Appearance, and Accomplishment	23
Listening and Talking	41
The Team	47
Promotions and Advancement	55
Self-Respect and Pride	63
Competition	71
Discipline	75
Instructions / Orders	85
About Crowds	91
Conclusion	93
Acknowledgements	95

INTRODUCTION

In 1920, Lincoln C. Andrews published "Manpower" – a loose field guide created to quickly train many inexperienced men for leadership roles after World War I. The book contained dozens of forthright leadership principles, many of which I believe could serve this century's new and existing leaders equally well, regardless of gender.

We again find ourselves shook by a pandemic, threats to democracy, and a renewed urgency to quickly train a significant number of people for new and ongoing leadership roles. Not to put us on a war footing, though future battles are likely, but to remind us of the central tenets and benefits of good and effective leadership, particularly in defense of democracy, and literally, saving the world.

Five Central Tenets:
1. Stay creative.
2. Have ingenuity in helping others become more efficient.
3. Build a stronger character.
4. Have a higher purpose.
5. Improve our democratic institutions.

Add to this, six leadership fundamentals.

Leadership Fundamentals:
1. The realization that every individual has a deep-seated desire to maintain their self-respect and be recognized by those around them.
2. Effective leadership is not autocratic. We are citizens of a democracy. If we wish to sustain it, we need people to be self-respecting, self-thinking, responsible, and capable of making and acting upon educated decisions.
3. Character counts. Personal character is essential to successful leaders. Keep your word, act with fairness, value human rights, and allow others to grow and develop.
4. People require self-control and self-discipline to consciously form positive, productive habits. Self-control is fatiguing compared to your nature; therefore, leadership must appeal to people's better instincts if one hopes to be successful.
5. It is crucial to remember that a leader is neither a savior nor a dictator. An effective leader learns the pulse and passions of those they lead, not through force, but superior preparation, experience, and ability. Swollen egos, pomp, and vainglory ruin new leaders.
6. A leader must be genuine. As a leader, you must appreciate your personality and the positive or negative effect it has on your team. You must be true to yourself, not an imitation of someone else.

Effective leadership is not a birthright; it is a chosen lifestyle that transcends paychecks and your life within an organization. It is about responsibility, fairness, and character. 'Welcome to Leadership' adapts century-old wisdom for today's new leaders because a renewed investment in good leadership is paramount to successfully meeting the onerous tests which lousy leadership has unfortunately left for us to urgently address over the next few years. The simple cure-all solutions offered by some are a pipe dream; we must all quit looking for the easy way out and instead get down to work. We must act as happy warriors, working efficiently, finding joy and satisfaction in the accomplishments of our goals, not in rhetoric or empty promises. You will play a positive role if you prepare to lead.

Welcome to Leadership.

LEADERSHIP PRINCIPLES

❖

This guide contains the practical elements and requirements of leadership. You may want to underline or highlight certain passages for future consideration and reflection. You are now a student of leadership, and the first step in executing any undertaking is to get a clear conception of the objective. People work better, and leaders lead better when the objective of their efforts is clearly defined in their minds.

The Objective of Leadership
The Objective of Leadership is to build up and maintain a high spirit of discipline and morale, individual initiative, loyalty, and teamwork, then direct this spirit to win the highest efficiency for accomplishing the purpose.

Therefore, every step's objective is to secure better discipline and morale, more intelligent initiative, keener loyalty, and better teamwork. The student of leadership must always keep these objectives in mind in both study and practice. Furnish a purpose or guide in all that is said or done.

Accomplishing these objectives is a constant inspiration to a true, good leader. Through comments and criticisms during the work's progress, they seek to build up morale and initiative and all the essential qualities in their team's characters.

Personal Qualities Required in the Leader
Effective leaders intelligently use the qualities that they already possess. This guide will not enumerate all the noble traits of the great leaders of history and then expect you to adopt them as your own. None of us have all of these attributes or any of them in perfection. However, all of us have some sense of justice and fairness, possess a degree of honor and self-control, and use our judgment and willpower.

The point is to learn the value of your various traits and to cultivate them through intelligent use. We are all human – admitting your mistakes and acting accordingly is an excellent first step toward leadership success. We are all human; therefore, treat others humanely.

Many people with mediocre ability have successfully carried through one big job after another simply because they had the faculty for inspiring their subordinates' loyalty, initiative, and best endeavors. Many others of stronger character and higher mental attainments have failed to do so because they could not inspire and/or perhaps outright antagonized their associates.

While their lack of tact may have been due to natural deficiency, more often than not, it was because they had used an antiquated notion about how to enforce discipline as their guide. Or, perhaps they never gave any thought to the importance of effective management. It is not difficult to learn how to avoid the mistakes of others and acquire the art of praising those who make enthusiastic efforts.

We are not discussing a superhero's high qualities or striving to attain a Lincoln level of leadership. Understand, not all these points will apply to every case of leadership. If you read something that strikes you as unreasonable for a circumstance you have in mind, give it a fair review as applicable to some instances, and weigh it as a means of adding to your comprehension of the true spirit of leadership. You cannot know too much about this in the general case. The broader your knowledge and the better defined your individual opinions, the better judgment you will be able to bring to your particular problems. You are a significant factor, and it will be what you believe, think, and feel that will make you successful or not. You will never win by following abstract rules that do not resonate with you and you do not live by.

Qualifying for Leadership
No one expects perfection, and it is impracticable to take on qualities that are not natural. You must realize that leadership is developed. Absorb its fundamentals into your system, and study yourself while applying them to your position's problems.

Your personality is the one big thing going for you. Learn to appreciate its strong and weak points, its possibilities for doing the right and wrong, and its probable effect on others. Get a handle on it by practicing self-control, and make it work intelligently per your wishes.

You will make mistakes — the best do. The point is to have enough sense to recognize the error, correct it, and avoid repeating it. Watch yourself, and observe others, always asking if the best thing was done to get the desired result. There is generally one "best thing" to say or do and at least a dozen wrong ones, and your chances of using the wrong one are strong. Still, by giving it thought, over time, you learn to pick the "right thing" until it eventually becomes instinctive for you. Think seriously about yourself in your job and determine that you will be natural, genuine, fair, and self-controlled. Realize that your team is made up of human beings influenced through your persona. Therefore, be determined to study your disposition and the tools to use your talents intelligently. Observation and reflections on leadership are great things.

No two leaders will act exactly alike because each relies on their personality. One may be naturally cold, short-spoken, and stern, whereas the other suave and gentle, yet both can be equally good leaders. When you analyze their team's treatment, you will find that both observe the same fundamental principles of justice, fairness, and regard for their individual development.

As the personalities of leaders must differ, so too will those of the team. To influence them, you must have a working knowledge of human nature — for while everyone responds more or less alike to well-known instincts and habits, there are times when you have to consider the individual. Here is where observation, experience, and reflection prepare you to act intelligently. If, as a leader, in any given case, you are not sure what to do, think what would make you respond cheerfully versus what would tick you off if you were in their place. Using this information, decide what you will do. It will generally be the right thing because, fundamentally, we are all pretty much the same.

Above all, you must be genuine. You must use your distinctive characteristics naturally and with an earnest purpose to play the game fairly. If, by nature, you are gentle and tactful, be grateful, and do not try to become a bear because you have seen and admired some big burly man who was a successful leader. The genuineness and earnestness of your efforts to do the right thing will go further than the best possible imitation of someone else, no matter how good they are.

Self-Control
Self-control is one step toward the ability to lead others, and you will more easily accomplish your self-discipline as you observe human nature. Note the blessings of the self-disciplined person and the curse to themselves and their teammates of those who are not. Parents who allow a child to grow up undisciplined put a tremendous burden upon the future community and a significant

handicap upon the person. Selfish, petulant, flaming into passion at any opposition, egoism coloring everything in life for them, make them a poor team member in sport and business. These types of people are more often tolerated by their peers rather than heartily welcomed. They have many hard lessons to learn before fully appreciating true values about themselves and becoming a contributing member of society. Far from being fit to lead others, they are generally the most challenging problem for the leader, who now has to do the work that the parents should have done in childhood.

You may assume that you have the requisite character for leadership, or you would not be in a position to use it. You will not prove your worth and improve your natural qualities by grandstand plays or prayer. You will accomplish it by continued thoughtfulness in meeting the human problems of your position and by self-discipline that will make and keep you fit for your duties.

Consideration for Rights of Others
It is good for every citizen to realize that they are part of a community whose members are entitled to some consideration. This aspect of community is important for the leader who is responsible for the conduct of others. Everyone hates the hog in sport, business, or community living. These types of people elbow women and older men aside as they crowd to the front at a ticket window and through a busy day, always jamming and trampling others to get the best for themselves. They gain satisfaction for their swollen ego but earn the scorn of their peers who have thought enough about life to realize

that this type of person has poor character and is a menace to the community.

Put Yourself in Their Shoes

Admit it; there are times you want to beat sense into a person. You could take potshots at them, leaving them sore and rebellious, or you could imagine yourself in their shoes. This allows you to express yourself in a way that can appeal to them and win them over, even if, as it often happens, they do not end up thinking they originated the idea themselves. The latter method is tactful — and compared to the former, gets tenfold results, not to mention adding to the joy of life for all concerned. Give attention to how you present ideas. Rather than concentrating on the idea alone, let them take it as they will. This requires some consideration of the other's probable feelings and thoughts, acknowledging their point of view, and how you would feel in their shoes. Leaders who have won a promotion from below have an advantage in having experienced their former peers' point of view, yet often disregard the prior wisdom by exhibiting a new-found swollen ego. Avoid this.

It is more efficient to be reasonably tactful and considerate. To do so, you may sacrifice a bit of vainglory and not appear to yourself and your team members as such a lord of creation. You will, however, get better results, make life more worth living for all, and build your respect in the eyes of others. The bigshot whose arrogance hurts the feelings of those less fortunate or forbids them to show respect and consideration to each person never does their appointed task well, no matter what capacity. This arrogance is found instead in the toad trying to make others think they are an ox. The humbler a person's station, the more likely they are to recognize a toad when they meet one, and the more pain it causes them to have to bow to its bovine pretensions.

Loyalty and Initiative

The leader is responsible for developing loyalty and initiative in their team.

Team loyalty is won by;
- gaining their admiration of the personal attributes you display,
- your commitment to the larger organization,
- your example, and by timely positive comments.

You develop their intelligent initiative by;
- the policy and methods you employ in handling them in their work.
- continuously encouraging individual effort, taking pains to commend every display of interest, inventiveness, ingenuity, or improvement.
- keeping the group informed of what it is trying to do as a whole, so each may understand the object of their particular part and seek the opportunity to do it better.
- telling the team what to do, not how to do it, and praise original effort and decision.

With constructive criticism and explanation, you encourage the team so that they want to do it better next time.

You encourage the team to observe, think, decide, and act on their decisions. So long as their spirit is loyal, the best results come from such service. The leader must be patient in developing these faculties.

Development of the Team's Powers
It is natural to be impatient with the person who is bungling their early efforts. Often the leader grabs the thing and does it themselves rather than wait for inexperienced hands to find the way. A young parent often says, "I'd rather do it myself than see them struggling with it." Similarly, this type of boss cares more about having a specific thing done precisely as they would do it, instead of their team member doing it, despite all the good that could come from their team's developed skills and resourcefulness. Of course, this method is wrong. Your way is not always the best way. One way is often as good as another, and improvements come from the worker's interested inventiveness. Your objective is to get your team's best efforts. Good work is not done in an atmosphere of humiliation and discouragement. You must avoid the natural display of temper at awkwardness and the cutting remarks, which indicate that you think the person is a hopeless idiot. If they really are, then you have a different problem and should avoid wasting your time and that of others to use them.

You are developing people and their capacity. Constructive and inventive instincts thrive in an atmosphere of encouragement. The opportunity to employ them keeps the team cheerfully at their task.

You get a double reward from this system of control; first, the satisfaction of seeing your subordinates grow their ability under your hands, and second, the satisfaction of increased output or accomplishment under your management.

POPULARITY, APPEARANCE, AND ACCOMPLISHMENT

Popularity

Should a leader strive for "popularity" with their team? Yes, if they can win it on their merits because it plays a large role in establishing loyalty. However, it is very easy for beginners to have the wrong idea of how popularity is won. You must clearly understand that it is not gained through easy-going methods, overlooking faults and neglects, playing favorites, sympathy with whining and moaning about how things have to be done, or in any of those things that undermine discipline and morale. Such popularity is cheap; it takes no effort to obtain and has no value once you have it. Such leadership is worse than worthless; it does actual damage and will be exposed as a sham the first time there's a call for endurance that tests the group's real grit and ability. Then one of two things will happen; failure or some better leader will jump out of the crowd, take the leadership from the weaker hands, and lead the team through the emergency.

The duty of all management is to discover and remove weak leaders. Equally important, every leader must study themselves and their methods to make sure that both display the qualities that justify holding their leadership position.

The popularity that counts is founded on admiration for your actual ability, confidence in your fairness and justice, and the courage and strength of your character. You win popularity with your team by:
- being fair and candid to all,
- seeing that both privileges and extra hardships are equitably divided among your team, holding everyone to a strict performance of duty,
- rewarding merit where due and acknowledging delinquency where it exists,
- avoiding anything like deceit or duplicity in your conduct of office,
- never appearing to ignore any of your team members as of no consequence in the group,
- showing a sincere personal interest in the welfare of your team as individuals,
- above all, the intelligent use of planning and forethought to save your team unnecessary work or trouble while increasing their efficiency, thus making them realize that you have the ability to lead them.

Appearance

The leader holds their position on the assumption that they are the best all-around person for the job out of the whole group. They must retain this reputation for excellence and should add to it by further performance. First of all, in appearance — in how you carry yourself before your team. The nature of the work may determine the amount of dignity which must go with the position. In every case, there is a certain dignity that all people must find in their leaders, to which they may instinctively give the leader their respect. This is about the amount of dignity that comes naturally from earnestness and sincerity of purpose. It is not a virtue assumed from superficial garments worn for work. It has nothing to do with haughtiness or stiffness. It simply comes from seeing things in their right proportion — big things big, small things small, and has more humility than pride. It forbids you to act patronizing or appear condescending to your team. Instead, you must share both their genuine concerns and their fun. The opposites of dignity are permanent solemnity and triviality — both of which can harm the human spirit.

Remember, you set an example with your appearance. Imitation is a great teacher — the sole teacher of our infancy, not to be despised in our role. Your team is going to act very much as you do — if you are really their leader. Your example of cheerfulness, promptness, loyalty to superiors, cleanliness, courtesy, energy, and interest will find a response in that of the team. The power of example is a potent force and instrumental in establishing loyalty.

An important example for you to give is the earnestness of purpose and interest in the work. The accomplishment of the work must appear to be a vital matter to you. If you are listless and indifferent, the team will quickly reflect those traits. Conversely, they will equally respond to a reasonable amount of smartness and earnestness on your part. You must appear to care so much for your work that you are indifferent to the little things that affect your comfort. If the team sees you taking advantage of your position to enjoy amenities denied to them, it induces a state of mind that interferes with good work.

Again, you want to impress upon the team that you are the one who knows right away what is to be done in each case that arises — the one who makes quick decisions and carries through on what you have undertaken without changing your mind. By figuring out ahead of time all the details of a certain undertaking and carefully planning for it, you can carry it through with an apparent readiness of decision and resourcefulness that will be surprising. A few such successes will establish your reputation as an able leader.

Knowledge of Details

Your position presupposes that you know the work better than any other person in the group. Generally speaking, you should be able to do each team member's part at least as well as the person in the role, know when they are working to their best advantage, recognize excellent performance to commend it, correct improper methods, and point the way to improvement.

This superior knowledge gives you the self-confidence to appear before the team as their leader and to provide them with reasonable instructions. Your crew instinctively feels and recognizes this authority and gives it respect.

Of course, no one person may reasonably claim to know everything or be more skillful in every detail than certain specialists. This fact is clearly recognized by the team and can be used to stir the pride of individuals in their particular superior performance. It can also be a reason for expecting everyone to make suggestions for any improvements they may have thought out.

Suggestions from the Team

As a good leader, you will encourage and give fair consideration to suggestions from the team. If accepted, give credit to the person; if rejected, tell them why it was not found suitable. It is a mistake to feel that you'll lose face in accepting or even listening to suggestions from team members. "Nobody can tell me how to run this job" is a narrow policy that destroys individual initiative — and it is not true. The very statement reveals the leaders who do not fully know their job.

The leader loses none of their prestige in hearing and considering the thoughts of their subordinates. In the end, the decision is yours, and on that, you have to act. It does not hurt your leadership to have to frankly say, "I don't know. I'll have to look into that." If you find that you have taken the wrong course, it does not hurt to admit that you were mistaken, especially if your action has resulted in injustice to one of your team members. Mistakes are readily forgiven; meanness or injustice is not. Always remember that people admire leaders with honor and demand justice from them. These qualities are better than infallibility because those you lead like to feel that you are human. Above all, they will not respect a bluffer. It is hopeless to try to bluff when you do not know. Someone will know and expose you, and away goes the respect of your team.

Asking Other's Opinions

Whenever one of your team members comes to you with a question or some trouble, make it a rule to ask, "What do you think about it? What would you advise doing?" They have probably been thinking about the issue for some time before they presented it to you. If it is a question about their work, they probably have a solution in mind, which they think is an improvement, and this is their way of getting it considered. By asking their opinion, you encourage their personal interest in the general success, enlist their cooperation, and ultimately allow that self-expression (which means a lot to every self-respecting person.) Not least of all, you gain time to consider your answer while they are presenting theirs. This is also an excellent way to handle a person's case brought before you for some failure of duty. Ask them what they would do if they were the boss with a team member who had committed the same offense. It is astonishing how this makes them realize the whole situation, which they probably had not thought of before. They will often suggest a more severe punishment than you would give and come out of the experience a much more responsive team member than before.

A Representative of Authority

In any business undertaking, the immediate manager of a group is to that team the direct representative of the authority which holds them to their tasks; the vision, goal, and direction which inspires their endeavors. They will get most of their impressions of this authority's justice and fairness from your behavior. They will judge the organization's worthiness from your enthusiasm and loyalty, and estimate your organization's efficiency by your daily display.

Management considered all this when it selected you as a leader; it is now for you to consider it constantly in dealing with your team. You must treat them fairly and wisely. They may depend on how your treatment impresses them for their conceptions of your management's fairness and the worth of your industrial life and institutions. It is up to you to make them content, useful, and happy — and not drive them to the ranks of revolution by making them believe that authority is unjust and your institutions unworthy of their loyalty.

The Head of the Family
A good leader is always a jealous guardian of the personal rights of their team. You do not allow an injustice to any of them individually, or the group as a whole. You are the team's champion in every contact with the larger organization, and the team looks up to you for it. In the modern society's multitudinous groupings, the individual chooses those groups that they believe offer them the best protection and give them loyalty. The leader takes advantage of this psychological fact when you make your team realize that you are always on the lookout for their interests. You may fight with them (in a caring way), but you do not allow anyone else to do so. You see that the team gets what is coming to them. If hardship has to be borne, you share it with the group and see that it is conducted justly. If resources are short, you do not rest until you have exhausted every effort to improve the condition and are very careful to not show yourself any favor. You fight for the team's fair name and full recognition of their merit. If one of your team members has trouble, it becomes your trouble until it is adjusted. You establish the feeling

that it is a family matter and that you are the family's head. (Incidentally, you are sure to be rewarded, for the team will soon be taking a keen interest in the welfare of the head of their family.) In the end, the group comes to speak of it as "our" team. Each realizes that their interests are equal in the effort with any others.

The Group Spirit

Any group of individuals working together for a common purpose will unconsciously and inevitably establish a group spirit of some kind. The leader knows that success largely depends on this group spirit and takes pains to make it a helpful one. By getting to know the team and "how they feel about it," you keep in close touch with the spirit that runs through them all. By providing suggestions here and there, you build it up and make the team feel a sense of membership. When you know this spirit well, you can count on your team to respond in a certain way to specific appeals or impulses, making this group spirit a tool in your hand for getting results. You play on this spirit to arouse new energy or endurance in times of hardship or strain, and tired muscles spring anew to life. Spirit may make teams endure and dare and carry through far beyond the everyday accomplishment.

The good leader is constantly looking for ways to build up this spirit in their group. By word and deed, and particularly by thoughtful conduct of the work in hand, you foster the spirit of putting things across and never being defeated, which will carry you through to success when called upon. Your team will come to realize that what you require of them is always reasonable and improves efficiency.

They find that you always consider their welfare before your own and take greater pride in your team's success. They come to realize that while you direct their work to make it as interesting for them as you can, you will never accept failure for them or yourself, and will insist on carrying through to successful accomplishment. It is possible to establish a strong team spirit for doing good work, and the team themselves will expose any laggards unfit for membership in the team.

Such results are possible to the leader in direct proportion to their knowledge of their job and their ability to conduct the work efficiently and without wasted time or energy. People naturally hate inefficiency. They become critical, caustic in their remarks, and finally disgusted under a leader who wastes their time and efforts. This type of boss hesitates over decisions and wonders whether to do this or that and how to do either, does not have the tools and materials right at hand, always picks the wrong person for an assignment, and delays the work of all. Such a leader will never build up any good spirit. Only the reverse of this picture of incompetence can accomplish that.

Work for the Leader
Leaders are not always right and sure in their management of affairs, but by looking ahead and preparing for each new task, you can ready yourself and lead your team with such an efficient direction that it will appear miraculous to others. Of course, this means work for you, but the notion that work grows less as one ascends the promotion ladder is foolish. Your task is not easy. Ambition for accomplishment,

pride in success, and the joy of meeting responsibility are the motives that hold the effective leader to their job.

Where Leadership Really Shows

As we watch a skillful manager directing their team through a job, tools, and material at hand, every person moving efficiently, all the parts working smoothly toward the result, it's natural to exclaim, "What teamwork!" and "What a leader!" This leader seems so good, not because they are endowed with skill, but because they have previously sat down and planned out how they would handle this particular job. They took pains ahead of time to see to it that everything was prepared for the work. Your superior leadership shows not in the work you are currently doing, but the work you did beforehand, building up your team's discipline, teamwork, and preparing for handling this particular job efficiently. That is why you may now appear so quietly sure of yourself and your team, and that is the real task for leadership — fitting self, individuals, and team ahead of time so they may work smoothly to the best advantage without waste or friction.

Assuring the Confidence of the Team

It is common for leaders to take too much for granted and assume that people understand conditions without explaining them. Remember that a person cannot provide good work if their mind harbors fear or distrust. Rather than alleviate this mental burden, many leaders are so poorly equipped that they instead inject additional fear and anxiety. The way to free your team members' minds and redirect them to more useful impulses is to provide them with printed rules and explanations that clearly define the policies and undertakings regarding administration and control. These rules include the rights, duties, and mutual relations of its members, and particularly the method by which each member may secure immediate attention from "higher-ups" in cases of real or imagined invasion of their right to justice and impartial treatment. In business, a person's distrust of their boss's impartiality and/or honesty is often justified. The vastness of an organization sometimes makes management forget its responsibility in discipline and fair treatment among its employees. Many frontline workers today find themselves in a case, not unlike that of our forefathers, who before us had to force a written acknowledgment of their rights from their tyrant king. These rights were so fundamental and straightforward that they should go without saying, yet they must be articulated.

Assuring Justice
The possession of authority makes a wise leader carefully consider others' rights, so they don't commit a grave injustice. Being unfair is likely to have a far different effect on the lousy leader of narrow soul and intellect. These types often become selfish, mean, arrogant, indifferent to others' feelings and rights, and partial to favorites they choose for selfish reasons. Thus, they deny justice and forfeit their right to leadership. As managers, these people are often the cause of severe troubles and are always the cause of reduced production. By deceit and duplicity, lousy leaders may long conceal their bad qualities from executives while also negating the most humane management policies. For this reason, when troubles show in any

team, first seek the source in their boss's defective leadership. For this same reason, successful management finds means to check up on the methods of its subordinates. It should be clearly understood that every person has ready access to a higher authority to present any grievance.

The Joy of Doing Work Well
People naturally get pleasure from doing well in whatever they put their head, heart, and hands toward. Whatever a person is doing in an agreeable frame of mind, they often find themselves naturally striving toward perfection. The joy from the fine execution of work results from an instinct and forms one of the best means for getting results if the leader knows how to use their instincts correctly.

When you see someone taking no interest in their work and not trying to get good results, perhaps even purposely doing shoddy work, you can be sure that something is fundamentally wrong. Some stronger instinct has been aroused whose force forbids the operation of this happy one for construction. Our strongest instincts regard our self-protection, and one of these may be causing the trouble. If conditions make the person fearful of their welfare, livelihood, or injustice, contrary instincts are likely to overcome or at least confuse the instinct to do well. So, we may expect superior results only under a system that assures fairness and justice under a leader who honestly practices them.

The Curse of Conscious Slugs

A common complaint is that by the end of your shift, you're too tired to do anything else that day. This is true less because of the amount of work you've done and more because of the small amount of interest and ambition you have been allowed to put into the work. People are happiest doing hard, productive, and good work if they can apply the right spirit. Unfortunately, many policies establish a standard of mediocrity that commits daily violence to the character of those capable, ambitious people who are forced to work consciously as slugs instead of being free to give their best. No wonder they are tired at night with no heart for outside interests. They are working in an environment that saps their soul and injures their self-respect as community members. You may see this evidenced in their slack, bovine faces as they soldier on in their jobs.

People often become interested in the success of their business and their undertaking. When no particular danger threatens or issue is at stake, a clever boss will appeal to the constructive instincts to make them dominate the self-protective ones.

Public opinion is likely to play an important part in this issue. The community is interested in anything that materially affects its citizens' character and its industries' output. It may decide and demand certain action that it believes will correct a situation it finds so injurious. And it may do this without a true conception of the facts. Far better, the leaders of both should solve their common problem for their common interest.

This issue must be a serious consideration for leaders. Only leadership that makes progress can last. Its purpose must be transparent, honest, and satisfy constructive instincts; otherwise, its following will seek some other endeavor that offers this satisfaction. While appeals to passion can carry people a long way in the short term, sooner or later, it is time for serious thinking. Then, these people must be convinced that their course makes progress and greater ultimate good. Unless the leadership has had a broad vision based on realities, the people will discover its fallacy or selfishness and abandon the organization.

Depending on a Person

You can make a person feel so trusted that their sense of pride and good sportsmanship will make them feel that they owe it to you to perform well. This strong influence on conduct can become too strong to be continuously used. It may quickly become burdensome to ordinary people, who generally want more freedom from the promptings of conscience. The point is to use your influence only in special cases, to reap good effect in results obtained and on the person's character. When you do use it, do so naturally and efficiently without too much fuss. There should be no obvious question of your confidence being justified — it is so sure that it is an unspoken understanding.

Ownership and Self-Expression

The leader should also take advantage of strong instincts for ownership and self-expression. A team member should feel that they have a personal interest in the job they are doing and that they are using their skill, inventiveness, and resourcefulness to actually execute a task. Watch for the chance and drop a remark to demonstrate that you see how well they have done regarding some step they have taken, and there is no harm if others overhear your remark. You will praise the way the person handled it and commend the excellent condition of their tools, thinking, or work ethic. By rewarding their little success and making it appear to be the result of their work on their job with their inner resources, you encourage the feeling that everyone is doing their work in their own way and will get credit accordingly.

These constructive instincts in the team have another meaning for you as their leader. If misused, they will cause the team to resent it when they find themselves doing useless work, wasting energy, and even approaching failure due to your poor judgment, hesitation in making decisions, and blundering through lack of forethought. This makes you see the necessity for knowing your job and carefully preparing yourself to handle its details.

Knowing the Purpose of Work

Human nature demands that before people can put their best efforts into work, they must know the objective. Purpose is the guiding motive in life, and we are made so that we seek the purpose in all our efforts. Upon finding it and believing in it, we naturally give it our best endeavors. One of the greatest faults poor leaders have in handling teams is that the team does not know what they are doing nor why. Understandably, a person must be interested in the task before applying much heart or intelligence. When you assign a task, ensure that the person understands the objective and its importance to the team's general work. That way, when the team is working, no matter how elaborate or challenging it may be, they can build a mental picture of the completed whole, see their part fitting into it, and employ their constructive instincts in making their part perfect. Clearly defining the objective of the work to others requires you, as the leader, to have a clear conception of the objective and enables you to hew truer to the line in carrying on the work.

Imagine two people each on a different day carrying buckets of water from a stream to dump into a tank on a nearby hilltop. One knows that every drop of this water is precious for the necessary irrigation of a garden they can see beyond the hill. The other has no idea why the water is carried — someone may be trying to dry up the stream for all they know. Not only would the former carry more water, but they would take more pleasure in their work and try to invent some way to increase the amount transported. When night came, they would be far less tired. This illustrates a truth that applies to all human activities. It is the leader's job to take advantage of this truth for the excellent effect it will have on your team and the work to be accomplished.

In starting any new work, undertaking, or policy, the most efficient thing to do is assemble the whole group of people concerned and explain to them what you and they together are going to try to accomplish. Explain each task and delegate them fairly. Finally, sharing a picture of success may serve as an inspiration or appeal to their reason.

Relationship Between Leader and Team
The relationship which should exist between the leader and their team is difficult to explain. It depends mainly on the leader's personality, and accordingly, you must work this out for yourself. This is frequently a matter of difficulty and embarrassment for beginners, who are apt to go to an unhappy extreme either in surrounding themselves with an atmosphere of isolation and autocracy or in showing too much familiarity and even frivolity. Remember, the leader is not an autocrat or dictator but the foremost of companions. This position puts responsibility and authority in your hands and a certain restraint on your relations' perfect freedom with others. You may still be called by your first name in perfect good fellowship, maybe even affectionately nicknamed. You may and should be in relationships of mutual and absolutely impartial friendship and confidence with your team, yet there must remain an air of authority and dignity which they recognize so as to naturally respect you and obey your instructions. You should be courteous and thoughtful for their interests but must never be patronizing.

If you take the time to observe, you will notice that a real gentleman or lady is always courteous to those in subordinate positions. The natural leader has no anxiety about their prestige and easily interacts with others. Those who bully them are showing that they have not had much experience in exercising authority. The true spirit of the American dream believes in the dignity of work. That spirit survives and makes it natural for us to respect those who do their parts well in whatever activity fortune has placed them. The leader and their team are companions in labor; each shows respect for the ability and accomplishment of the other and the team as a whole.

That is the spirit of the relationship between leader and team by which you regulate your conduct. You can see how this spirit is sure to be offended by exhibitions of pompous authority or childish familiarity. Team and leader are both entitled to the serious consideration of the other and respect in direct proportion to their demonstrated ability in performing their part on the team. Each will be judged by this test.

LISTENING AND TALKING

Take Time to Hear Team Members

The leader must have time to listen to their team. You must not be too busy to take up a matter any one of them may bring to you for consideration. It is easy to look important and say, "I haven't got time," but each time the leader does it, you drive one more nail in the coffin of the team spirit whose life you should be cherishing. Lousy leaders decline meetings because they fear they do not know the answer. It is far better to make the person feel that they were right in coming to you and listen to their proposition, even if, in the end, you have to admit that you do not know. You must have time if you want the loyal cooperation of your team. It is more challenging and unproductive to force the frank, timely expressions you need than to avoid being bothered by too many of them.

The busiest leader can and should arrange their schedule and policy so every team member knows that they may personally see them if the occasion warrants. Let everyone know that anyone having troubles is to bring them directly to you, and the problems will rapidly diminish. Your time will be repaid in added efficiency.

Talking to The Team

There is a surprising amount for the leader to consider when talking to their team. Currently, you may not talk enough, or you may talk too much. You must explain the objective, organization, and policy of any new undertaking to everyone. By doing so, you get better results and save a lot of talking down the line. On the other hand, a reputation for continually sounding off or lecturing will practically ruin you. A leader should observe the rule of not speaking unless they have something worth saying (and that nothing is worth saying unless it is worth being listened to.)

The habit of talking without demanding the close attention of those supposed to be interested is bad business and will cause trouble and misunderstandings later. Yet, many leaders are guilty of this and expect to continually repeat their instructions before they are understood. This is partly their fault and partly that of the listeners — but the leaders are responsible for both. In the first place, the leader must talk directly to the point. If you don't have this ability, you must train yourself daily. First, think about what you have to say, even precisely how you will say it; then say it and stop. You will not talk as much, but it will go farther. People are so unaccustomed to saying things that count that they become embarrassed and confused when they find themselves the object of close attention. You must meet this, for holding the team members' close attention is an important part of your responsibility in talking successfully.

Demanding Attention of All

When you have anything to say to one person or many, get full attention first, and insist on having it while talking. You often see the impossible situation of a leader making remarks that they consider important and members of their team not paying attention, even engaging in side conversations. When you have to talk to several people, call them around you, in a setting where you can see all their faces and as near to you as practical so you may speak in a conversational tone, if possible. You will have to give this constant attention, for the devil prompts some people to always slip around behind you, while others always take the most distant seats and await your invitation to come forward. Once the team members are in front of you, you can make sure that your points land. If an interruption occurs, immediately stop talking until all can give attention again. If your remarks are for everybody, everybody should hear them, and you are responsible for what they do. Make that a rule, stick to it yourself, and you should have no trouble.

Talking to Individuals

When talking to an individual, try to be so clear and definite that you will not have to repeat yourself. Let it be understood that you expect such attention from them that repetition will not be necessary. Of course, sometimes you may have to deal with people untrained in concentration and who may struggle to retain information. You will have to be patient in making yourself understood. The meanest type of mind keeps thinking of what it will say when it gets a chance while you are talking and gives your remarks just enough attention to note when a pause comes so it may begin to speak. This kind of behavior is a curse in any walk of life and not to be tolerated. The art of listening is a valuable one. Everyone should cultivate the habit of concentrated attention to what is being said if it means anything to you.

Example Better Than Talk

In the line of not talking too much, it is worth remembering that Napoleonic addresses do not arouse the American spirit before the fight. If the leader wants keenness and enthusiasm in doing a piece of work, they arouse this by example. Actions speak louder than words in this capacity. You cannot put your team members on their toes by telling them that you want them there; you must bring the follow-me spirit to work and put so much positive energy and vitality into it that your enthusiasm is contagious. By keen direction, happy suggestion, possibly a bit of competition, and most of all, by example, you unconsciously put your team members on their toes and hold them there until the task is done. Then, you may all talk about how good it was and share the credit.

Proper Subjects for Talk

There are things that you must talk about. Your subordinates must understand your methods and policies because you want their cooperation in carrying them out. Remember that while you are dealing with intelligent people, they are not wizards able to divine your thoughts. Do not assume a manner of aloofness and superiority or wrap yourself and the work in an atmosphere of mystery. Explain, in candid, plain, one-on-one talks, about what you are getting and how you intend to get at it. The atmosphere you want is one of mutual understanding and confidence. However, you do not get it by saying you have it, but showing that you have it in how you treat the team.

Another subject for you to explain is the spirit of discipline, its objects, and its necessity. Many team members have never thought about it, never realized the need for obedience and the advantages of cheerful obedience, never heard of teamwork, or thought of loyalty to teammates. As occasions arise, you can explain these things to make them interested in the very real influences on the team's conduct. In this way, you may do much toward building up the group spirit that you want. If rules are violated, it is often possible to explain to all your team members how the offense damages the group's discipline as well as reputation and thus get better results than you would from inflicting punishment.

From time to time, explain the larger organization's affairs and reiterate your mission statement. Tell them anything to increase their knowledge of the whole scheme and their interest in its success, for both these add to loyalty and morale. You want team members to have the stimulation that comes from a genuine interest in the general result, keep the cards on the table, and make team members participants with you in the development of the work. We all need to be shown, but we jump in heartily once we understand what is wanted.

Talks by the Big Chief

The head of any organization gets far better results when they assemble all their leaders and talk to them about their policies, plans, and how things are going in general. The day has passed when the source of authority is supposed to be clothed in awe-inspiring majesty and commands of servile obedience. The chief who denies close relationships to their subordinate leaders, who does not take them into their confidence and let them know their plans and how they propose to carry them out, creates the suspicion that either they are not sure of themselves in their job or that their plans and purposes will not come to fruition. The effective executive does not fear scrutiny and seeks cooperation and suggestions. Today's successful business leader makes themself the captain of a team whose members cooperate intelligently for its success. For this reason, the leader brings everyone together, shoulder to shoulder, so they feel fellowship in a common cause, where they all get the inspiration of their leader's leadership to grow enthusiasm for the leader's hopes and plans. Filled with a common purpose, everyone returns to their tasks. Each is better aligned and more highly determined to play their part to the larger organization's best advantage. Before a significant change, the most successful leaders take time and pains to explain in person to assembled groups of their managers to go about the general plan of the coming action and the exact part each particular group plays. There is no effort at oratorical appeal to passion, simply recognizing the ability and willingness to do their full part.

THE TEAM

Reception of New Team Members

The ultimate success of a new person joining a team depends, of course, on their character. But much can be done to hasten their success. The practice of the ages has been to haze the newcomer, but this is not approved in modern practice, which aims to get good results quicker through encouragement and by *showing* them *how* rather than ridiculing them for not knowing. Both schools of training have their adherents. There is something to be said in favor of judicious teasing to remove tendencies that might interfere with the new person's progress, but the difficulty is to make the ribbing good-natured and avoid overdoing it or doing it where not helpful.

This becomes another care for the leader, who must see that each new person gets the right start. Most new people want to do good work, so encourage them along that line and try to prevent anything that will switch them to the other track. To most newcomers, an early exhibition of your friendly personal interest in how they are coming on will be a great help and incentive to better work. There will be many things that they do not understand and some real or imagined troubles. This is your chance to establish a relation of confidence in which they form the habit of bringing these troubles to you for a solution, instead of letting them rankle in their minds and act as deterrents to the good impulses for work. This gives you many opportunities for improving the group spirit and may someday be the means of clearing up genuine grievances, which might otherwise lead to serious trouble.

The new team member's future depends largely on the start they get, their first impressions of the organizations' spirit and policies, and the habits they form. The smarter they find the team to be, the more pride they will take in belonging to it. The closer attention they are forced to give to the exact performance of little details, the sooner they will get the habit of doing things precisely right, and the sooner they will become a helpful member of the team. You can teach new tricks to new people more quickly than you can to old ones, whose well-formed habits you must break before implanting the new ones. New team members are a valuable asset to a good leader, for you can come nearer, making them the kind of team members you want.

Mutual Acquaintance Among Subordinates
Another important thing is to assemble the team in a way that they will get to know each other personally. They are partners in the same enterprise, and a knowledge of each other's equations is indispensable to their successful teamwork. Personal acquaintance and, even better, friendship will add tremendously to their efficiency. The various departments of an organization are generally interdependent. A team member will give quicker and better attention to another team member's needs if they know each other,

especially if they respect each other. The leader should make occasions for getting their subordinates together in friendly personal relations. They will be pleased to find that they all speak pretty much the same language, though some may not have thought so before. This closer association removes the affectation of some and the extreme humility of others and exposes them all for what they are — fellow members of the same purpose, equally sincere in striving for its success, and equally to be judged on their sole merits of performance. It is sure to be of advantage if the management goes into it with sincerity of purpose.

Supervision of Workers

The leader's job is one of supervision and direction. Your business is to see that each team member does their part to the best advantage for the general result. When you know the individual capacities of your team members, you can confidently assign the right person to each task. As with all the other leadership duties, this requires you to continually observe your team's individual performances, commending, correcting, and coordinating their efforts. This prevents you from actually taking part in the work yourself, not because it's beneath your dignity, but because becoming involved in doing the actual work distracts your attention from the duties of supervision. Many things could be going on without your knowledge. When the boss shows themselves eager to use the pick or shovel, some are always willing to lend them the tools and watch their efforts with assumed interest.

There are always some members of the team who need to be held accountable for their work. For the leader to allow them to get away with shirking their parts of the task would naturally cause chagrin to the others. The leader is responsible for the spirit of teamwork, which requires that each person feel sure that all the others are equally faithful in doing their part, and you must therefore see to it that they are. Of course, conditions may arise when the task is unfamiliar or peculiarly difficult. The leader may jump in for a minute to show the team members how or to set the pace — but do not put yourself in as an actual performer of the work.

Choosing People for Tasks
The duties of a leader frequently require you to be picking people to do assorted tasks. In your team members' minds, this is always a test of both your ability and fairness — and you want to prove that you have both. You do this by picking the right person for the job — the right person not only because they are the best qualified, but because everything considered, it is best for the team that the correct person be chosen. This requires the leader to know their capacities and attitude and to keep track of their conduct and work. Each group generally has individual cheerful, willing souls who seem to invite the task. The leader who is unsure if their orders will be obeyed always picks one of these team members to avoid the possibility of disobedience. The shiftless leader picks one because it is the easiest path. Both are wrong. They fail in fairness, and, by putting extra work on the more willing, they put a premium on being mean-spirited and injure the group discipline. They would do better to choose the lazy or sullen ones for the extra work, thus putting the

premium on cheerfulness and showing that they had a sense of justice and an ability to run the team.

Cheerfulness, Your Responsibility

Understandably, team members cannot do good work in an atmosphere of gloom. Elastic muscles, alert minds, superior energy, and endurance come from cheerful spirits and happy hearts. It is unfortunate if a group does not contain at least one indomitable soul who will joke and uplift the group through hardships and far more remarkable accomplishments. Yet, some lousy leaders sacrifice this with surly, inconsiderate, dominating control to keep their team members sore and heavy-hearted, discouraged with themselves and the work, and indifferent to results. These lousy leaders create an atmosphere of impenetrable gloom and then expect the impossible in demanding good work. Cheerfulness and hopefulness must always emanate from the leader. No possible hardship or obstacle may justify your failing to radiate these helpful qualities. Your character must be too strong and resourceful to be overcome by obstacles; and too confident of your team members' excellence and their ability so as to cheerfully overcome obstacles. Some days will test your courage, physical fitness, and vitality to do this, but you must give of your spirit to put spirit into the team, and by the sheer force of your cheerful dominance over the adversity, lead them through to a happy conclusion.

Permissible Growling

A certain amount of growling and whining to let off steam seems good for the soul and should not be denied to your team. You may ignore it, make light of it, and even sometimes get a good laugh out of it to clear the air. You do not, however, indulge yourself in it around the team. Do not tolerate any of it if it resembles disloyalty because it will undermine morale. You must know your team members so you may use good sense about taking their vaporing's too seriously and still prevent anything like real disloyalty. As members of a group, people can lose much of their individual responsibility and become more or less like children. You must consider this when judging their real feelings as they talk together.

Such situations require a level head and a knowledge of the team's true spirit — and are interesting tests of your qualifications as a leader.

Loyalty by Example

One of the leaders' primary things to develop in their team is loyalty; loyalty to you, the team, and the broader organization. You demonstrate the power of your example in cheerfully carrying out the instructions from a higher authority. If you are told to do something disagreeable, do not try for cheap popularity by saying to the team, "so and so has ordered this, and we have got to do it." Accept your full responsibility and take your team through the work. Your team is a part of the larger group and should play its part therein as loyally and keenly as you want the individuals to play their roles in your team. Try to arouse their pride in having their team do its part well, their interest in the larger group's success, and their belief in its leader's ability.

When to Question Instructions

If you have an honest question of the fairness or wisdom of the instructions, go to higher authority first and fight it out yourself in the interests of your team, without any question of loyalty. That is part of your business both as a guardian of your team's welfare and as a loyal member of the larger organization. It is a delicate matter involving your sense of subordination and your judgment about what is best. Do not do it with a blustering attitude, but quietly, in a spirit of loyalty, respect, and desire for the whole's best interests. Such action is infrequent — if your larger organization is in reasonably good hands.

Receiving Instructions

When you receive instructions from a higher authority, be sure you get their true meaning before you begin to act. Take time to understand, but do not quibble about minor details or fuss about how the instructions are expressed. You are expected to use your sense and ingenuity in executing these instructions, so be sure that you have grasped their spirit and purpose. Then, go to their execution with enthusiasm and loyalty, which will carry the same energy to the team.

How to Encourage Suggestions

You now know the value of encouraging team members to make suggestions for improvements and how they can increase efficiency and the pleasure in their work by trusting their constructive instincts and their natural desire for self-expression. So, how are these suggestions to be encouraged? Not by superficial methods.

The suggestions you want will spring naturally from the interest and partnership you have made the team feel in the organization. From the ideas for improvement, they then evolve as they carry on at their work, thinking how it might be done better or how they might get more significant results. The only encouragement they need is this atmosphere of partnership; and a boss who has a sense enough to give their suggestions fair consideration. The leader who has no time or patience to listen to suggestions will never get the team's best efforts and is doing the enterprise real damage.

Every person should feel certain that their suggestion will be fairly considered. If the idea has real value, they will be given full credit up the ladder. The way to do this is to take the individual in person to a higher authority and have them personally explain their idea. This performance makes their importance as a member of the team very real to them and their peers. If in a large business concern, the person was called before the board of directors to explain the details of some improvement they had thought out, nothing could do more to establish a sense of partnership in the undertaking. Appreciating their value, you can make as much as you will of every opportunity to increase the team's interest in the work and their sense of cooperation.

PROMOTIONS AND ADVANCEMENT

Advantage of Ambition

Ambition for advancement is another human instinct to consider, both connected with your career and handling your subordinates. Everyone should feel that they may progress as far as their actual ability warrants — and they certainly may, for good leaders are still rare and desired. The truest saying of life is that there is plenty of room at the top. Selfish ambition cannot win. The unselfish ambition of an individual improves both their chances for promotion and the work of the team. Industrial progress and individual advancement both spring from individual efforts to increase output or decrease energy expenditure. It is generally true that the great stream of intelligence, inventiveness, and adaptation flows from the bottom up and not from the top-down and that the top is continually being recruited from the bottom. This is so common a fact that it is frequently overlooked. It is so wholesome a fact, so characteristic of our democratic institutions, and so helpful a thought in times of unrest and discouragement that it should be emphasized and frequently brought to mind.

Never Deny an Earned Promotion

An earned promotion should never be denied to a person when their opportunity comes, simply because their superior feels that they cannot spare their services. As unjust as that is, it is often done and always to the detriment of the team spirit. In reality, very few people in life are so crucial to their positions that they cannot be replaced. No matter what pains are necessary to train the person's replacement, it is far better to let them go than it is to keep them and lower the morale of all by showing that your selfishness or laziness will stand in the way of a deserved promotion. This situation is often avoided by the excellent rule that each person in the organization shall always have at least one other qualified to take their place.

How to Win Promotion

There are numerous ways to win advancement, and plenty of resources are available to find suggestions on this topic. These are general hints: A person does not triumph by bragging about their abilities or by anything that smacks of arrogance. The way to get a superior's attention to your merit is to make the merit conspicuous. Management is always seeking the person who can produce and that superior results will soon catch their eye. Go at each task cheerfully, and above all, make it clear that your one significant interest is the organization's success. One thing that often denies promotion to a good candidate is the sentiment from their superior that, yes, they are good, but it's all about them 90% of the time, and the team only 10%. This is too bad when the same amount of work and ability unselfishly directed might so easily have carried them ahead.

Value of True Merit

The saddest thing is to see a person get disheartened and quit trying because they think their merit is not recognized. Make the merit big enough, and it is sure to win.

Someone will find out and buy your superior services. Ralph Parlette explained this in "It's Up to You," in which he illustrated human experience by what happens when you shake a jar containing a mixture of beans and nuts: The little beans rattle down, the smallest to the very bottom and the larger nuts shakeup, the largest to the very top. Thus, we find our place and hold it in life's struggle, according to not only our wishes but to our actual size. Friendly influence may elevate the little bean to a high position, but the jolts of experience soon rattle it back to the place it fits without rattling; adversity may have crowded the big nut to the bottom, but the same jolts will see it shaking up again to the top. It is not luck that takes one up or down; it is size — and the answer to ambition is to grow bigger. "Everybody wants to go up. But everybody is not willing to pay the price by first growing bigger so that he can shake higher. So many want to be boosted up. Everybody is doing one of three things: holding his place, rattling down, or shaking up. Whatever place we shake into, if we want to hold our place, we must hold our size. We must fill the place, for if we shrink up smaller than the place, we rattle. Nobody can stay long where he rattles. And you observe that to hold our size, we must keep on growing enough to supply the loss by evaporation. Evaporation is going on all the time, in lives as well as in liquids. A plum becomes a prune by evaporation. I wish human plums became as valuable when they become prunes."

Joy of Accomplishment

Akin to one's natural delight in doing things well is the motive for accomplishment, the pleasure one gets from seeing a thing completed. We all know people who are more or less ruled by this passion and aren't interested in anything else until they finish what they started. The satisfaction that comes from accomplishment is often cited as one of the best feelings in life. This may be enjoyed by every individual no matter what occupation. It means the satisfaction to be had from accomplishing the tasks in our own daily life and work.

A good leader often appeals to this instinct to increase accomplishment. It helps explain the advantage of letting the people know what they are doing as they work, especially letting them know from time to time what they have accomplished toward the general result. This is why the posting of progress charts does so much to arouse interest in the progress of the work and is another reason for including the frontline in a knowledge of the general progress of the whole organization.

Everyone is supposed to have an underlying purpose, some goal in life. But we do not have to await the satisfaction of having attained this distant goal. We get more satisfaction en route from the successful completion of each of the small steps that bring us nearer to the goal and count it as a good day if we have taken a step or two in the right direction. The leader may encourage the faith and assure their subordinates' continued efforts by showing them from time to time where they have made successful progress toward the desired end.

Indifference and Discouragement

If indifference and discouragement, the natural enemies of our drive for accomplishment, are allowed to invade our minds, they can seriously prevent this instinct's operation. They are born from failure, or what seems like a failure when long-continued efforts show no results, and from getting stale through the constant repetition of the same task, without variety or the stimulation of new ideas. The leader must combat these enemies by introducing other thoughts that are more constructive. You must encourage the discouraged and interest those who are bored. You may often stimulate interest in even monotonous work by commenting on the perfection of its execution and the amount of its daily output. For example, it is possible to relieve the monotony of long hours at the same tedious machine by letting two people alternate tasks if it can be done without offending the sense of ownership, which makes a person resent having another touch "their machine." Here is the leader's chance for ingenuity. You know what is needed; it is up to you to supply it. Possible suggestions include; Learning other jobs to help with promotion, brief opportunities for supervising others' work and getting better acquainted with the general work of the whole organization.

Justice, Fairness, and Surplus Spirit

Justice and fairness are the first essentials for handling people successfully, yet we often see leaders who give them no consideration. Human nature demands fair play and gives its best response only in that atmosphere. We have to recognize that our best advances in civilization and community living have been based on a philosophy that acknowledges how the natural impulses of humankind react to fair dealing and decent treatment.

Successful organizations run on the fundamental proposition that ninety percent of humankind are good and will do good work when confidence is shown in their good intentions. Their organization's working rules are accordingly made to fit the significant majority rather than the ten percent minority. Unfortunately, in many organizations rules have generally been made to fit the few weaklings who are not strong enough to play fair, while the significant majority have had to be cramped in their freedom because of the ignorance of these few. This common problem in organizations is distinctly arbitrary, unjust, and indicates unfitness for leadership.

This same spirit of indifference to the good people's well-being in making efforts to control the shiftless is found in every business and walk of life. The point is that better results are obtained by showing confidence in good intentions, allowing more freedom of action, and controlling the meaner spirits through education, elimination, and the spirit and example of their coworkers. Remember that fitness for good leadership is proven by arousing an enthusiasm that makes people want to give their all. It is not shown by control through arbitrary methods. Any fool can create rules which practically reduce their people to a state of serfdom.

You will encounter all kinds of situations in which to show fairness. It is impossible to anticipate them with rules, but you may be successful by practicing continued determination not to act in passion or impatience and to judge each case fairly with consideration for all. In doing this, you will arrive at the best solutions. Remember that your final decisions must help develop individual character and group discipline.

Occasionally there are people of so much virility of body and spirit that they cannot expend enough of it on the ordinary day's affairs, and the surplus often gets them into trouble. A good leader tries to accommodate them with enough hard work and play to keep them comfortably steady. In contrast, the poor leader, blind to human nature, punishes their faults without effort toward remedy and gives them a reputation for deviltry and even for worthlessness. Yet these very people were capable of tremendous exertions for good had they been properly directed. Giving people work to keep them out of trouble is wise, simple, and is well worth remembering when you find somebody looking for trouble. It is a well-known trick to call up the energetic person who is always getting into mischief, arouse their pride by finding an element of their personality to praise and rely on, and subsequently put them in charge of a committee or team, eventually leading to the potentiality of promotion. Nine times out of ten, they will react to this responsibility by providing exceptional service. The challenge is finding the right opportunity to promote a seemingly difficult person and not establish any unfortunate performance standard for winning promotion. Isn't leadership interesting?

SELF-RESPECT AND PRIDE

Self-Respect Essential

The leader has to guard their self-respect and that of their team. Self-respect is essential to having self-confidence, and self-confidence is essential for both you and your team members to play their part successfully. If work is to progress efficiently, each will be continuously called upon to decide what is best to be done and act upon them without hesitation. Therefore, each must have enough self-confidence to do this without running to someone to ask what to do to pass the buck of responsibility.

In the Leader

As the leader, you must maintain your self-respect in your daily contact with life, your team, and your office's conduct. Your relations with your superiors and peers; your knowledge of your job; your self-control of temper, frivolity, pettiness, etc.; your methods of directing work and handling people are all to influence and are evidence of your self-respect and are matters for your consideration. You must realize that you stand before your team as a more capable person on the job than any one of them. In this light, you want to be an inspiration, not an apology. It needn't lessen your self-respect if you lack physical stature or age and long experience, though both may be helpful. Superior knowledge and moral qualities determine one's fitness for leadership and enlist the team's loyalty and obedience. It is not the body's size, age, color, or gender, but what emanates from the soul that makes the leader.

In the Team

The leader must cherish their individual subordinates' self-respect. You need their intelligent cooperation and must often depend on their judgment and willingness to carry on without specific instructions. If your team does not believe in themselves nor feel that you believe in them, they will be afraid to decide what to do and be scared to do it for fear of failure and consequences. By showing confidence in them, by never ignoring them as individuals, by encouraging and commending good and correcting an error, you develop your team's self-respect as a sure basis for the self-confidence and strength of character you need to meet your requirements.

Courage, Fear, and Self-Control

A leader is likely to be called upon to meet emergencies requiring a cool head and a stout heart in many fields of activity. Many people shrink from assuming leadership responsibilities because they lack the nerve and show fear when tested. Everyone feels fear; it is an instinctive warning of imminent danger or threats to our well-being, and we are self-protective creatures. The purpose of this warning is to make us take steps to meet the threat and lead us to action. We soon forget the fear, as it generally disappears when we have sprung into action. A developed mind and character, bodily health, and a determined purpose, all combine to help to avoid showing fear or letting it improperly influence our actions. No one willingly follows a leader who lacks a courageous character, nor could a leader hope to succeed if they were self-conscious of their moral weakness. Both the leader and their team must have confidence that the leader possesses courage and force of character to be self-controlled and capable of calm, reasonable judgments in crises. The leader establishes this mutual confidence through self-control and sound judgment during the smaller emergencies of daily life. If you bellow and shout because some little thing goes wrong, you not only fail in self-control, you make your team question your character's force and ability to meet a serious crisis. Therefore, new leaders should make a point of training themselves in self-control under trying circumstances. Seek situations that test your nerve and judgment rather than avoid trouble as the weak person does by quietly slipping away.

Control by Power of Example
The leader's function is to be calm in an emergency. Remain unruffled, even sardonic if you have it in you, in the face of hardships. Be unperturbed and even casual in the face of danger. If you are a real leader, your team will take their mental attitude from what yours appears to be. In danger, they will watch your movements, even facial expressions, for reassurance. It is then that you drop a casual remark or do some simple thing naturally, showing that you are at ease and confident in these abnormal circumstances. In this way, your team regains their wavering

confidence, feeling that you are not afraid. In times of unavoidable hardship, you must avoid showing annoyance or impatience. Your sarcastic acceptance of necessary conditions will unconsciously lead to theirs. This saves you from the morale crushing, grumbling, bucking, and cursing out everything in general. In an emergency, you must show perfect self-control. Remember that your conduct will determine that of your team. (If you are excited, they will be more so.) An emergency will call for accurate, determined, self-controlled work. If your heart has jumped into your throat, made your voice quaver, and your ideas confused (this happens to the best of us), nothing but disaster will result if you communicate all this to your team. You will gain time and success if you take time to swallow your heart and regain perfect self-control before you say anything to betray your perturbation. Then, give your directions with a calm, self-assured demeanor of a real leader. Directions given this way are a great comfort to the team and assure steady, intelligent execution. To begin shouting excited ill-advised instructions in an emergency is one of the most characteristic failures of inexperienced leadership. Train yourself to be one of the exceptions by acquiring the habit in any given situation of being sure of yourself and then calmly giving directions to your team.

You have the opportunity to train for this in the ordinary affairs of life and acquire a facility for knowing what to do in an emergency and doing it with calm assurance. There is generally an admirable bystander whose mind has acted instantaneously in any public accident or emergency, who has jumped in and done the right thing.

Question your mental processes to learn why you were not the person, and try to qualify next time.

Decision

Successful leaders stick to good decisions that do not have to be changed, while the valor of ignorance is to make quick decisions that are generally wrong. Of course, quick decisions are preferable if they are right. A good leader typically takes time to weigh the subject before deciding. In many cases, it is best that you take the time to consult your team first. But in every case, you must ultimately come to a decision as to your course of action, announce it clearly as your decision, and have the force of character to carry it out without showing hesitation or vacillation. It is insufferable to depend on a leader who cannot make up their mind, or those who have come to a decision then allow themselves to constantly waver in the face of each new thought. If you have any of those tendencies, eliminate them by watching your decision-making process. Practice in the minor moments of your daily life, cultivate your power to grasp the essential facts of a situation, arrive promptly at a decision, and stick to it despite any trivial matters that may come along to make a change seem better.

Value of Thinking

The more you think about your job's details and possibilities, the more you keep your mind on your work, the better you will be prepared to make good decisions quickly. "Because I am always thinking about it" was Napoleon's answer when asked how he was able to make such prompt, accurate decisions in the art of war. In business affairs, the leader who is a thinker, who thinks of the business at hand and is mentally prepared to meet its demands for direction, will do best.

A leader should be so resourceful and confident of their judgment that they successfully meet these occasions for a quick decision. You can get a reputation for this ability by carefully planning ahead of time for specific tasks and making quick decisions during their execution. To maintain this reputation, you must acquire the habit of giving thought to your work, not only in anticipation of specific outcomes but continually as the work progresses.

Personal Pride
Pride is another quality of human nature that is very useful to the leader in managing their team. Pride is primarily established by seeking out superior accomplishment cases within your team and promptly commending your subordinates. Once developed, pride becomes an influence that the leader can use for better conduct, better results, and patient endurance of hardship. You will not get it in a day, any more than you will get discipline or morale. It comes from the performance of good work that has been recognized and rests in a justified feeling of ability and worth. Do not expect to get it by simply announcing to your team that they are the finest. Bring them to honestly believe in their value through your recognition, praising their good work, and making suitable remarks to outsiders, which some of them may overhear.

Find something in which they excel, and brag about it moderately. If possible, find a way to show their ability publicly. If your team can get a reputation for excellence, good people will seek to join it, its personnel will improve, and it will continue to grow better.

Pride in Organization

Pride in the organization has a tremendous influence on keeping the team on point. It makes them keep each other up, and you begin to reap the rewards for having established it. You see them developing the spirit of discipline you had hoped for and the cooperation in that teamwork, which means so much to everyone involved. Every leader should always strive to arouse this pride. Your ingenuity and the practical use of your knowledge will help people take delight in doing things well and in having their excellence recognized. The excellence of the individual should be reflected in the reputation of the team and out of the bodily and mental development which comes from consciously doing things well, which helps to grow self-respect, laudable pride, and assurance which strengthens the individual character. These are the elements of the organizational spirit which you should seek to establish in your team.

COMPETITION

Competition Affecting Individuals

The instinct of rivalry or competition, which makes a person strive to excel among their companions, is another tool at your disposal. This is so powerful a motive that it has to be used with good judgment. Once launched in a real contest, most people are likely to sacrifice anything to win. As a general rule, what you want from your team is a high average of performance, which can be maintained without any impairment of their powers, so you must judge the case fairly before introducing the contest's spirit. You must not use it eternally to keep the team on edge, but only on worthwhile occasions. There are moderate things for which it may be used regularly to stimulate effort, make the best record for punctuality, etc., but you would not want a person to be driving himself constantly to capacity. With this said, use your judgment to guard against individual injury as well as to keep the spirit fresh for use on real occasions.

Team Competitions

Competition between teams engaged in similar undertakings can increase results and bring each group's individuals into close cooperation so that their team may win, giving them a better comprehension of the spirit of teamwork. As every leader is continually trying to develop their collaboration, these rivalries are very common. But where your team competes with another in the same organization, it must play fair as a larger team member. The same rules of cooperation and loyalty apply to the conduct of your team here, as to the individual members of your team at home. You may not do anything for your team which injures the other team or lowers the esteem of your team. "Sure, they're good, but we can beat them" is the proper mental attitude for contests within an organization.

Care of Your Team
Looking after your team's welfare is an essential part of the leader's direct responsibilities. Each job presents its problems to be solved according to the conditions. The big thing here is to realize that your team's welfare is an important consideration for the leader who expects them to do good work. It would seem unnecessary to state that a person's mental and physical fitness has much to do with their accomplishments. Yet, so many bosses appear indifferent to a person's condition as long as they can drag themselves to their work. In reality, you must investigate whenever any person shows a letdown in their performance. A person cannot keep up good work on an empty or sour stomach, nor give continued careful attention to details if some trouble is constantly intruding on their field of consciousness. Knowing that sore feelings, grievances, and mental troubles interfere with good performance, the intelligent leader does all they can to eliminate them. If you don't keep your team in the best

possible physical and psychological condition, you are throwing away all kinds of potential energy; running a six-cylinder engine that is skipping many of the cylinders.

Two opposing considerations should be kept in mind when looking after your team's welfare. You are to build up their self-respect, initiative, individual responsibility, and self-determination; therefore, you must not patronize them, coddle them, or treat them like children. On the other hand, you have to recognize an individual's characteristics in a group. This need for oversight is true in every activity. The leader has to be on the lookout to see that their team does the necessary things for their comfort and welfare.

You must understand all the facilities offered, their advantages, what management intends each resource to do for the team — and stay in close touch to see that the team gets the right ideas and makes the most of those resources. But beyond all that, in the sole hands of the immediate manager are the thousand simple things of the daily work and play in which the thoughtful leader makes their team feel their interest in their welfare, success, and happy living.

DISCIPLINE

Creating and Maintaining Discipline

The inexperienced person is likely to have more apprehension about their ability to maintain discipline than about anything else in connection with taking charge of a group of people. Due to their inexperience, these types of people wonder if others will obey and are not sure of themselves as a disciplinarian. It helps to get a fair idea of how discipline is maintained. Discipline results from the leader's whole conduct of themselves and their job, personality, methods, and everything they do for their team and themselves. Among all these, rewards and punishments play an important part. Rewards have a great deal more to do with building up discipline than punishments and are given much more easily and pleasantly. If the leader has established the right environment, they will rarely find occasions to use any punishment. With all kinds of teams, in every phase of human endeavor, fair treatment and the encouragement that comes from the judicious appreciation of good intentions and praising good work soon establishes a spirit that makes punishment out of place and unnecessary.

Discipline from Rewards

A very effective reward is the slight word of recognition of individual effort or excellence; sometimes, even a nod and smile work wonders. The main thing is to show this person and the others that you see and appreciate what they are doing. As you supervise the work of your team, be on the lookout for chances to commend individuals. Do not overdo it; fulsome or unmerited praise does more harm than good. Keep it as intended, an acknowledgment for excellence that every person likes to receive. Your team will naturally strive so long as they feel appreciated in what they are doing.

One leader will inspect their workers, look only for faults, and speak only to criticize something as wrong, while another will seek good work to commend it and correct mistakes in a spirit of improvement. The first may hold their team to a certain level of accomplishment; the second will soon have them all going in a spirit of emulation. One does not see why they cannot do as well as another one next door, whom they heard the boss complimenting. Appreciation of a person's excellence appeals directly to one of their strong instincts. It never fails to inspire continued effort to win further praise.

Influence of Good and Poor Leaders

In every group, you can find certain, cheerful characters who make the best of things, joke with the rest through the demanding tasks, and whose influence is a great asset. The leader must note these people and do what they can to increase their influence with others. If you have to show favor to someone, pick one of these people to receive it, thus letting everyone see your appreciation of their cheerful, willing spirit.

On the other hand, there are often certain people of the meaner sort. They do the whining and complaining for all, and their influence is in the direction of lowering the group's morale. You must be aware of these individuals and do what you can to convert them to cheerfulness and a will to win. Where a person's influence is poor, be sure you do nothing to strengthen their standing with their teammates. If someone must draw a disagreeable task, it is often a good idea to let such a person have it as a reward for being such a downer.

You must know your team and watch their work and spirit, so you reward the deserving and never appear to support the undeserving. When your team's morale is being tested in times of hardship or strain, it will win through or break down, depending mainly on which type of people have a stronger influence. In this case, it will pay off if you have strengthened the hands of the strong, cheerful ones and made them subordinate leaders of sentiment and opinion in your group.

Leader a Maker of New Leaders
One of the finest things about being a leader is the chance it brings to build up character in others, discover their difficulties, weaknesses, and possibilities, and help build a stronger person and better citizen. Taking a keen interest in your team's personalities and making it your business to build up a reasonably strong and useful character

out of what may have appeared an almost hopeless wreck of humanity brings great satisfaction and a personal feeling of reward that you are making the world a little bit better.

Every leader is, consciously or unconsciously, constantly affecting the future of their team. Your power to reward and punish makes this true. Your decisions and acts of authority tend to build up or discourage the character of the person affected. To see this power of leadership in the hands of ignorant, unscrupulous, brutal, or even thoughtless people is shameful. The good leader realizes how strict fairness, encouragement, and guidance develops their team's powers. Continued injustice will break someone's spirit, destroy their dignity, and leave them a worse member of the community than it found them; a strong leader accepts this responsibility and takes pleasure in using their power for the better good of the team, the community, and the work at hand. These types of leaders are makers of new leaders in some measure, and with that thought in the back of your mind, study problems with a desire to solve them.

Discipline by Punishment
Punishment is a severe word to use with ordinary daily affairs. Still, there is no milder word than "punishment," whose meaning fits the case. Not typically used, it stands only as a last resort. The penalties of the law stand in the background as matters of no personal interest to law-abiding citizens. Yet, those penalties and the means for administering them are essential elements of community organization. They must be intelligently understood by those responsible for community welfare. In this respect, the leader has the

same responsibility to discuss how they will use this power of punishment to meet this responsibility successfully.

The intent of punishment is to be corrective. It must be administered for the sole good of the person and the group and never in a spirit of vindictiveness or revenge. Punishment represents all the corrective measures commonly used to discipline people — reprimand, docking pay, deprivation of privilege, suspension, discharge, etc. The severity of any given punishment is mostly a matter of the spirit and infrequency it is given.

It is possible to fix a set standard of punishments, but this standard cannot be followed arbitrarily, as that would ignore the significant human factor and all manner of extenuating circumstances. Every case of an offense must, in fairness, be judged on its own merits. As the leader, you must evaluate the peculiar circumstances, consider the offender's personality, and above all, discover the underlying motive. It is unquestionably true that most people naturally prefer to do right and go wrong only for some reason. Very often, a sense of offended justice is behind the wrong-doing. In any case, the punishment cannot be reasonable unless founded on a true understanding of the facts. It must be both reasonable and just, for its one big object is its effect on the team member's character and the group discipline. This effect is the determining factor. The leader and team must both always realize that whatever punishment is given, it is done for the good of all and that of the individual.

Investigation of Offense

To get at the actual truth of the matter takes tact and knowledge of human nature. Develop this ability in yourself. It will be challenging to convince someone to be frank because they may not quite believe in your desire to be fair. Their instincts of secretiveness, pugnacity, being a good sport, etc., all stand in your way. Putting yourself in their place is a good rule during the investigation. Finding truth will take time, patience, and skill until you have established the tradition of honesty and fairness for all. Avoid ever acting in passion and instead always show a determination to get the facts to judge fairly. You will soon be able to get to the truth about each offense and learn what it means in your organization what this person has done. Then you may decide what steps to take for the best interests of all.

This type of leadership is not utopian, nor does it take too much time. It is a leader's role to have time for these things — and you save time by doing it thoroughly. Soon, you will discover how to root out the cause of soreness and trouble and establish a spirit of fairness and decency that will reward you with freedom from having future offenses to handle.

Actual Punishment Unnecessary

While every offense must be taken cognizance of, not every offense has to be punished. It may often be made the subject of a plain talk to all of the team. Explain what the offense means to the organization's success and put it firmly that a better result may be obtained without punishment. Do not feel that punishment must always follow and fit the crime. Use your common-sense judgment, and do what you believe will best promote the discipline you are trying to inspire in all. A reprimand with an explanation of what the offense means to discipline is generally punishment enough.

The Leader's Responsibility
If, in the end, you decide that punishment must be given, give it yourself. Be very jealous of the authority over your team; do not let anyone interfere with it or exercise it for you if you can help it. You want your team to look to you for justice and see in you the seat of authority under which they act and to which they are responsible. This means that you must personally handle every case and make it clear that the decision as to the punishment is the result of your judgment. If the offense must be punished with more severity than you are empowered to administer, then send it to a higher authority along with your recommendation.

Prompt Action Necessary
Rewards and punishments on the individual and the team should be taken immediately after the incident while still fresh in everyone's mind. Let your team realize that you are effective at managing and that the conduct of each is a matter of great interest to you. Overlooking offenses and willful negligence may cause offenses to multiply and discourage faithful workers. The word or nod of recognition of good work is immediate and effectual, as does the first step in recognizing or correcting an offense. This first step may be an admonition or even a reprimand where you are sure it is justified. But the first step is generally to call the person up and ask their

reason (in a tone that assumes they have a reason) and that you intend to give it fair consideration. You may have to defer action for further investigation, yet, you have still taken the first step and received the immediate effect.

Symptoms of Poor Leadership

We have all seen people in positions of authority who are examples of awful leadership. A little authority in their hands appears to upset the balance in their heads. They lose all sense of how to deal with people, become ridiculously arbitrary, loudmouthed, and blustering. They try to rule by putting the fear of God into others, by strength and brute force. They are the boss because they have been named the boss, and they will show you. When they see anything going wrong, their first step is to bellow, "what the hell are you doing?" in a tone that implies that the person in error is not only a fool but a criminal. They assume their motives are those of a thief and a liar — and then expect them to respond with good work and loyal service, which is, of course, ridiculous. Such methods of control bring sullen obedience and invite open revolt. Swagger and bluster are but a thin camouflage for incompetence, and it would be a wholesome thing for these leaders to be able to realize the scorn and disgust they are implanting in the hearts of their team. Some don't know any better and may be made good by training; others lack strength of character and may be hopeless. Neither should be left in authority as they are.

Misconduct — Fault of Leader

Where you find recurring cases of insubordination or indifference of good work, you will generally find that the cause for it lies in the presence of a leader who is not good enough for the job. People typically start any job with good intentions. If many things go wrong on a team, the answer is assured that there is something wrong with its leader. Likewise, where leaders find themselves unable to maintain discipline, they may seek the cause within themselves. When you hear statements like, "I've got the worst team. No one could do anything with them." it is an admission of the leader's unfitness. People run about the same, are subject to the same instincts, and are controlled by the same general principles. The same group of people who were all but anarchists under a hard-headed, narrow-minded manager can become one of the best-disciplined teams of the whole organization under a few weeks of new leadership, which embodied fairness, principles, and decency in handling people. The lesson is straightforward to the person who wants to be a good leader and the employer who wants their managers to get good results.

INSTRUCTIONS / ORDERS

Giving Orders

Beginners question in their hearts whether they can get the team to obey them or not. Perhaps this is the first time in your life you have ever been in a position of authority to give orders. Maybe, you have never enjoyed the habit of command and, unless carried along by a dominating influence, are ill at ease in giving orders. This is very common with new leaders and calls for experience and training before making good. If a "newbie" by tone or manner betrays that there is any doubt in their heart that an order will be obeyed, it invites disobedience. Common exhibitions of this uncertainty are; the sickening apologetic tone and words, high-pitched shouting of the order, accompanying profanity, repeating the order again and again, and threats as to what will happen if it is not obeyed. These are all sad exhibitions of inexperience or incompetence and are sure to lead to trouble. Avoid every one of them and school yourself in the correct methods — the following are some suggestions.

How to Give an Order

Do not give too many orders; give as few as possible. First, make sure that the order is necessary and that the thing to be done is reasonable. Secondly, pick a suitable person to do this particular thing, and call this person by name to get their attention. Thirdly, in a quiet tone, give them your instructions, like a baseball manager tells a team member to cover third base. There is no question of obedience, no thought of it. Your quiet tone does not assume that the person is deaf, a surly dog, or a criminal. Assume that they are an intelligent, loyal member of the team of which you are the captain. It will not occur to them to disobey such an order.

How Not to Give Orders

You will stimulate disobedience if, by tone or words, you insult your subordinate's dignity, question their loyalty and obedience, or by threats, dare them to disobey. We see this often illustrated in daily life, where people untrained in authority are required to exercise it. Generally, giving orders in such a manner will stir up trouble rather than gain cheerful compliance. This reaction is undoubtedly true with most holders of a brief authority.

Sometimes it will feel as though some have gotten the idea that amenability to instructions is proportional to the noise produced in giving them. When every order is roared at the team and generally accompanied by a volley of profanity in a pathetic effort to exercise authority, it is an astonishing exhibition of not knowing how to handle people. Naturally, it does not command respect or conformity to the team.

Disobedience may often be the direct result of how the instructions were given; remember this when investigating a case. While that may not justify your overlooking this particular offense, it should enable you to correct the cause of trouble and avoid continued offenses. Teach the subordinate to give orders correctly, or you may have to take away their authority.

The Why of an Order

Where possible, give the reason for an order while you provide the instructions. This enlists the person's intelligent interest in carrying them out and gives them a chance to do better work because they understand the desired result. Of course, there are occasions for quick and simple action when this would not be reasonable. Never apologize for giving the order. It must be clear that you are explaining what is to be done. Give the reason for the action only when it is clear that the circumstances warrant it and when it will lead to better results.

Necessity for Following up Instructions

Equally important as giving instructions is to see that they are executed. This does not mean that you stand glowering at your team member until they move. Go about your business in absolute assurance that they are carrying on, but if they fail, be sure to note it and take action. Too many leaders feel they have done their full part when they have given the order. To overlook even slight neglect is likely to lead to more serious ones. For a person to be guilty of direct willful disobedience is a very serious thing in any organization. It threatens the discipline of all and demands drastic action. Do not let it be true that you have gradually led a person into disobedience through your shiftless leadership, whether due to your laziness, ignorance, or lack of nerve to enforce your authority.

Make it a rule of the organization that whenever a person is given a particular task, they are expected to report back as soon as it is done. You can see the advantages of this compared to assigning a task to someone, then letting them feel as if you have no further interest in the said task. The designated person realizes that you will know how much time they took and the significance of the task. Additionally, you realize that your duty is not entirely done when the instructions are given. It gives you a chance to check up on their execution and to praise their speed or excellence. It provides the person with an opportunity to try to win this praise. For example, better results are achieved when giving a child a particular task if a parent says, "let me know when you are through."

Willful Disobedience
Regardless of everything on your part, you may still be met with a case of direct willful disobedience, which conditions outside your knowledge or control may have caused. If you want to handle this case wisely and save the person to the organization, you must realize how their mind is working and act accordingly. They are concentrating their faculties in opposition to the latter channels of obedience; therefore, you have to focus them on the task of breaking out this channel of disobedience. To win them over, you must first

divert their faculties from this concentration by requiring them quietly to do a simple thing like handing you an object or adjusting their clothing, anything that you are quite sure that they will do for you. Then by easy stages, you develop a state of mind that will make it possible to discuss the original trouble reasonably, thus regaining control and saving them from grave consequences. It takes patience and a high order of leadership to save a person in such serious cases, but you will find joy in executing the task. Any fool can fire a man; you want to do better than that.

Orders Rarely Necessary
In general, the better the leadership, the fewer the orders delivered. Teamwork, cooperation, initiative, loyalty, and intelligent leadership development make orders mostly unnecessary. Things are done in response to suggestions and carrying out instructions as to what is to be done.

We may envy the leader whose team will jump in response to their quiet, firm tone of command, but do not imagine this to be magical. They have developed a strong character and a knowledge of human nature in practical school, learned that self-control is the first step in managing others and that teams respond in kind to the treatment they receive.

The Tone of Voice
The tone of your voice, not only in giving orders but in all your verbal intercourse, is worthy of your consideration. It is a potent

element of your personality in its effect on others and is easily within your control. It may interest you to the point of regarding your inflection hereafter to realize the critical part that human speech has played in our development from pure animalism. Language is the foundation, as it is the agent of all knowledge. Even so, we continue to see examples of people so blind to this importance, so indifferent, that they allow themselves to roar, growl, whine, or chatter in close similarity to other animal species. Others bungle the use of their voice deplorably; it causes one to shrink inwardly from their rasping one. People attempt to win others' minds and yet speak in tones so repellent that convention alone makes us stay to listen. It is a pity they do not think to hear themselves as others hear them and thus learn not to sacrifice this natural asset longer. For half the power of speech is in the tone.

We all recall cases where it was the tone of voice that caused the trouble. "It wasn't so much the thing he said; it was the way he said it" has caused many people to argue forcefully. But it is not alone in making trouble that the tone of voice can accomplish so much.

The cool, quiet tone of a leader bringing order out of chaos and re-establishing control and confidence among excited people is impressive. As is the virile animated tone putting pep into one's work and the firm, confident tone that wins an obedient following even through danger and hardship. The power of speech is tremendous — use it to your advantage.

ABOUT CROWDS

The Mob Spirit

You may have occasion to deal with the "crowd spirit," or even the "mob spirit," so it is wise to have some idea of how these things come about and are controlled. In normal circumstances, individual community members are law-abiding and self-restrained in deference to public opinion and their sense of responsibility. Some sense of common wrong may unite certain ones into a group for the common purpose of obtaining redress or instituting improvement. "Mob mentality" may start with no intention of committing any overt act or even doing any particular thing, yet end by being led into most unfortunate excesses.

Individuals in Crowds

The individuals who compose the group have, to a degree, lost their identity and have passed much of their individual responsibility to the group's shoulders. They then come to find themselves feeling free to do things they would never consider doing as individuals and being controlled by statements and suggestions, which they would know to be absurd in ordinary circumstances. Then, they approach a point where they do not respond to sound reason and logical argument but instead react to impulses aroused by passionate appeals, daring suggestions, almost anything that has a catching sound and is repeated often enough. Thus, they may end by becoming a mob, susceptible to blind impulses, and ruled by unreason.

This group is easily amenable to control in its beginnings, for the "mob will" has not yet taken form, and the individuals still retain some sense of reason, personal responsibility, and fear of consequences. But the longer they remain together, the greater their numbers, the more they are harangued as a body having a common purpose, the more surely this crowd will take form and make possible their transformation into a mob. Therefore, by temporizing with the crowd, you strengthen its unity and encourage the growth of its concerted will. Action to control the situation must be prompt and decisive in order to direct the crowd's immediate dispersal. It may be controlled only by similar tactics to those of the demagogue who now leads it or by using the armed forces of the law. These are points well worth the consideration of every citizen, whether they contemplate joining a mob or trying to prevent one.

CONCLUSION

You may be wondering how this guide failed to mention so-and-so as one of the most important elements in leadership. Hopefully, you are because in doing so, you have taken a big step in leadership in that you have yourself considered and weighed its requirements. Only by giving personal thought to reflection and deciding upon your methods and conduct will you succeed in handling others. Let your purpose be clear and worthy, and your policy based on fairness; be yourself genuine, unselfish, and just; make your team partners with you in the enterprise. Through your personality, admit your team's loyal cooperation and following; keep in mind that your objective is to increase their power through their developed individual character, and then work out the details as your own experience and judgment dictate.

Good luck.

ACKNOWLEDGEMENTS

In 2020, when I discovered Lincoln C. Andrews's "Manpower" had become public domain, I read it and was immediately struck by how history repeats itself, especially if we don't pay attention. "Manpower" was published in 1920 after a punishing war, a horrific pandemic, and in a time with bountiful threats to democracy -- a different yet familiar theme 100 years later. It struck me how relevant many of the leadership elements outlined remained and how others appear to have been lost and forgotten.

The tone reminded me of the conversational style of my much beloved maternal grandfather, James Ellard, "Grampa Jim," and the content made me reminisce fondly about leadership conversations with my father, John Bimshas.

My goal for "Welcome to Leadership;" update the language to make it palatable and respectful to a diverse audience of new leaders while retaining the "old-fashioned voice" of another age that often compels us to listen intently.

It became an unexpectedly challenging task. I resisted the urge to strike some phrases that no longer worked because I wanted to stay faithful to Andrews's original words. Constantly weighing the verbiage of each passage stymied progress and my enthusiasm. My son, Karl Jonas Bimshas, a senior in high school at the time, provided clarity by urging me to fish or cut bait on the project, I suspect mostly because he was tired of hearing me complain about my self-induced dilemmas.

Thankfully, Jenny Swartz brought her editing skills and perspective to bridge the gap between the language from the past and present.

Unbeknownst to each of them, this eclectic team coalesced in my mind to help produce this adapted work. Much thanks to them all.

ABOUT THE AUTHOR

Karl Bimshas is a Leadership Advisor and prolific author. Boston-bred and California-chilled, he earned an M.S. in Executive Leadership from the University of San Diego and a B.A. in Mass Communications from Emerson College. He has held several operational and sales positions in public and private corporations.

Ready to manage better and lead well in your organization?

At Karl Bimshas Consulting, we advise busy professionals on essential leadership development and accountability skills so they become confident, competent, and valuable leaders in their field without becoming jerks.

Visit KarlBimshasConsulting.com

www.ingramcontent.com/pod-product-compliance
Lightning Source LLC
Chambersburg PA
CBHW052332220526
45472CB00001B/389